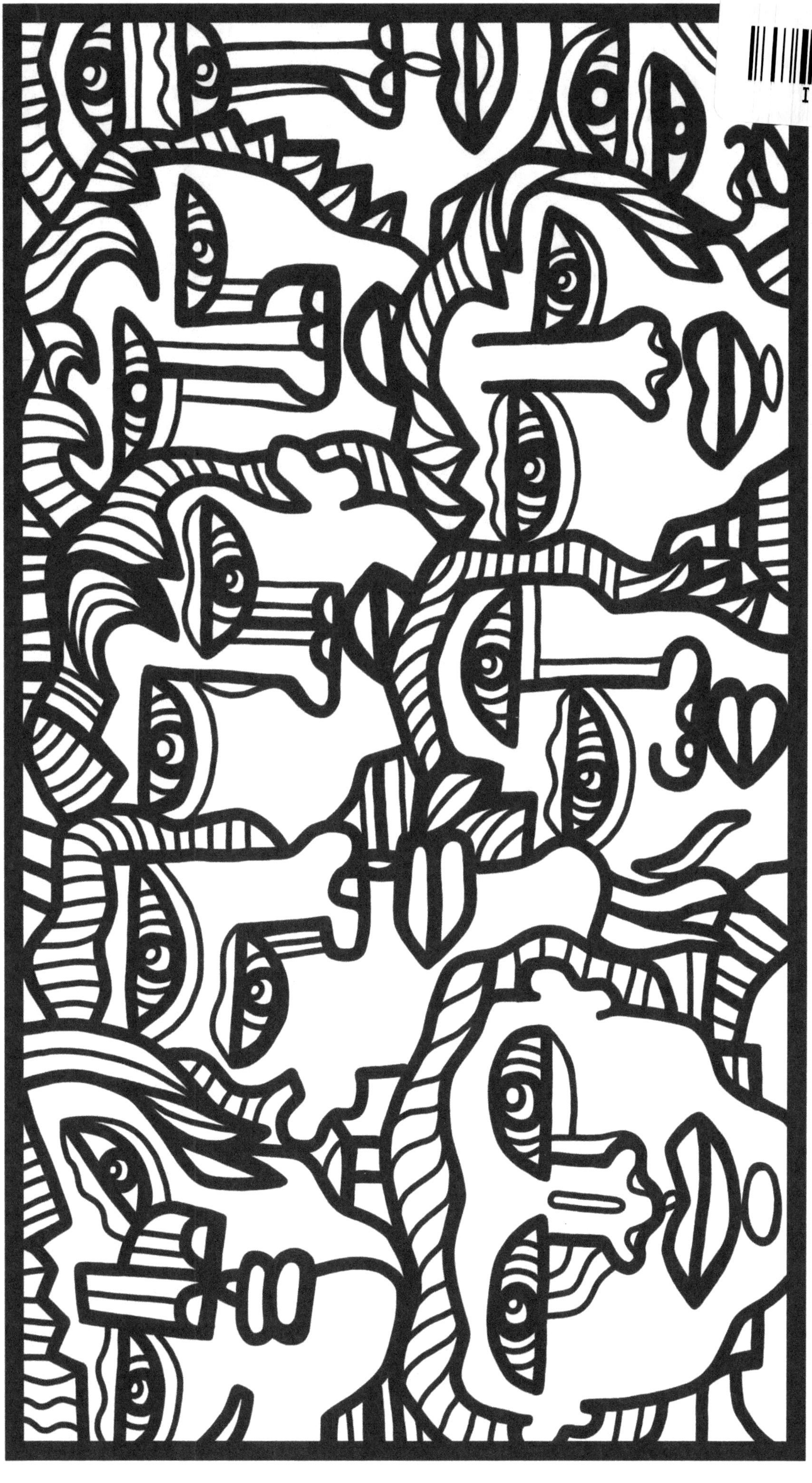

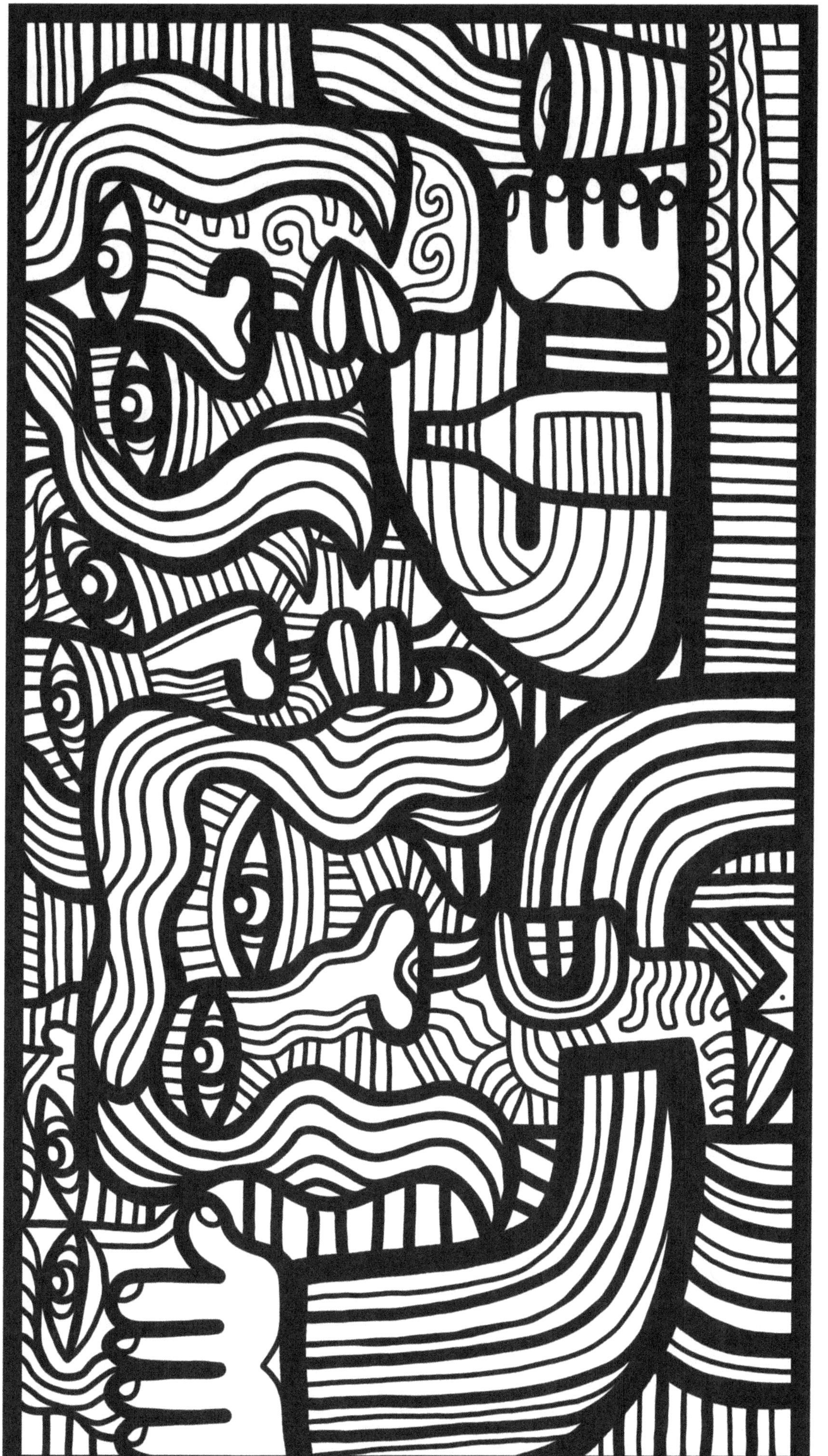

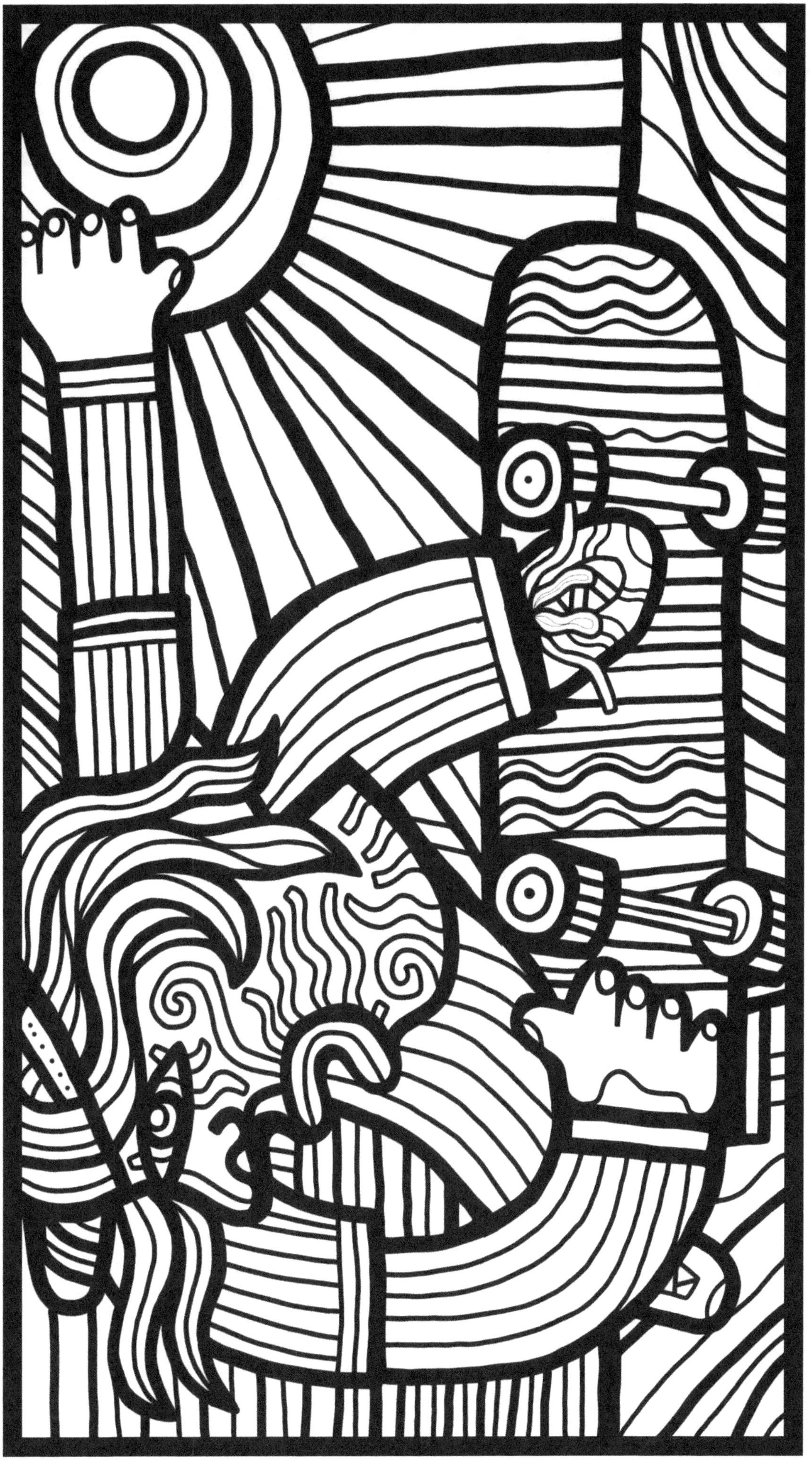

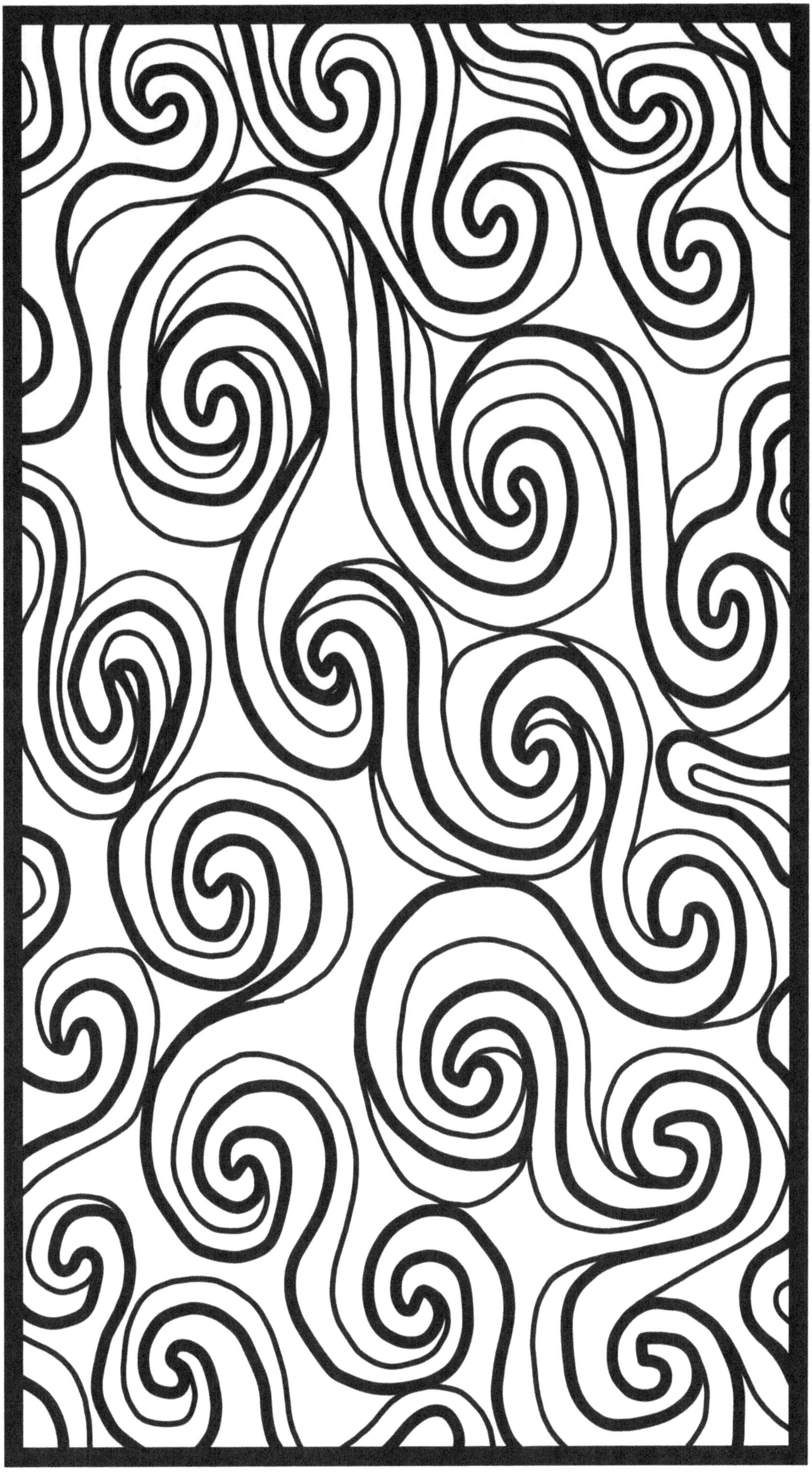

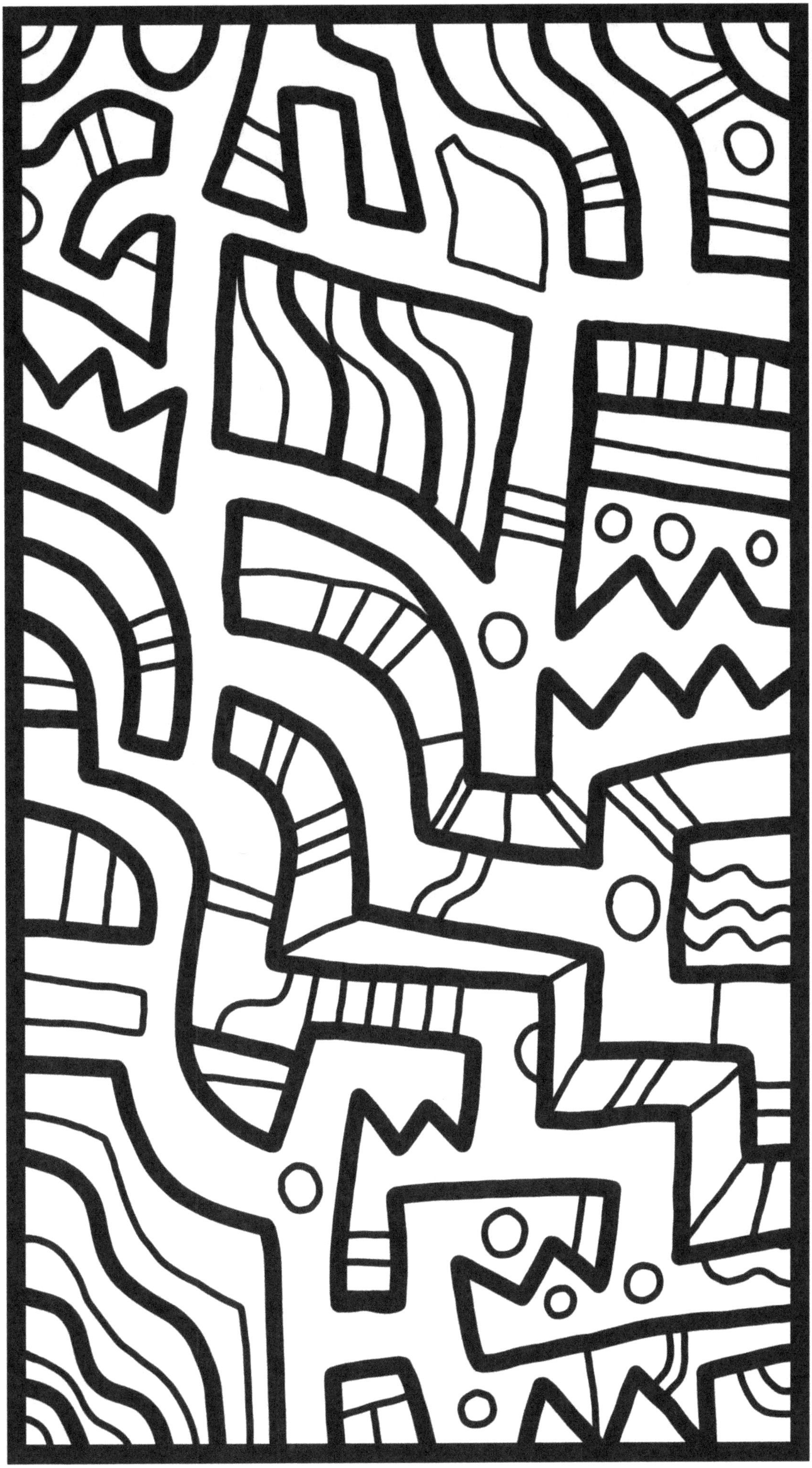

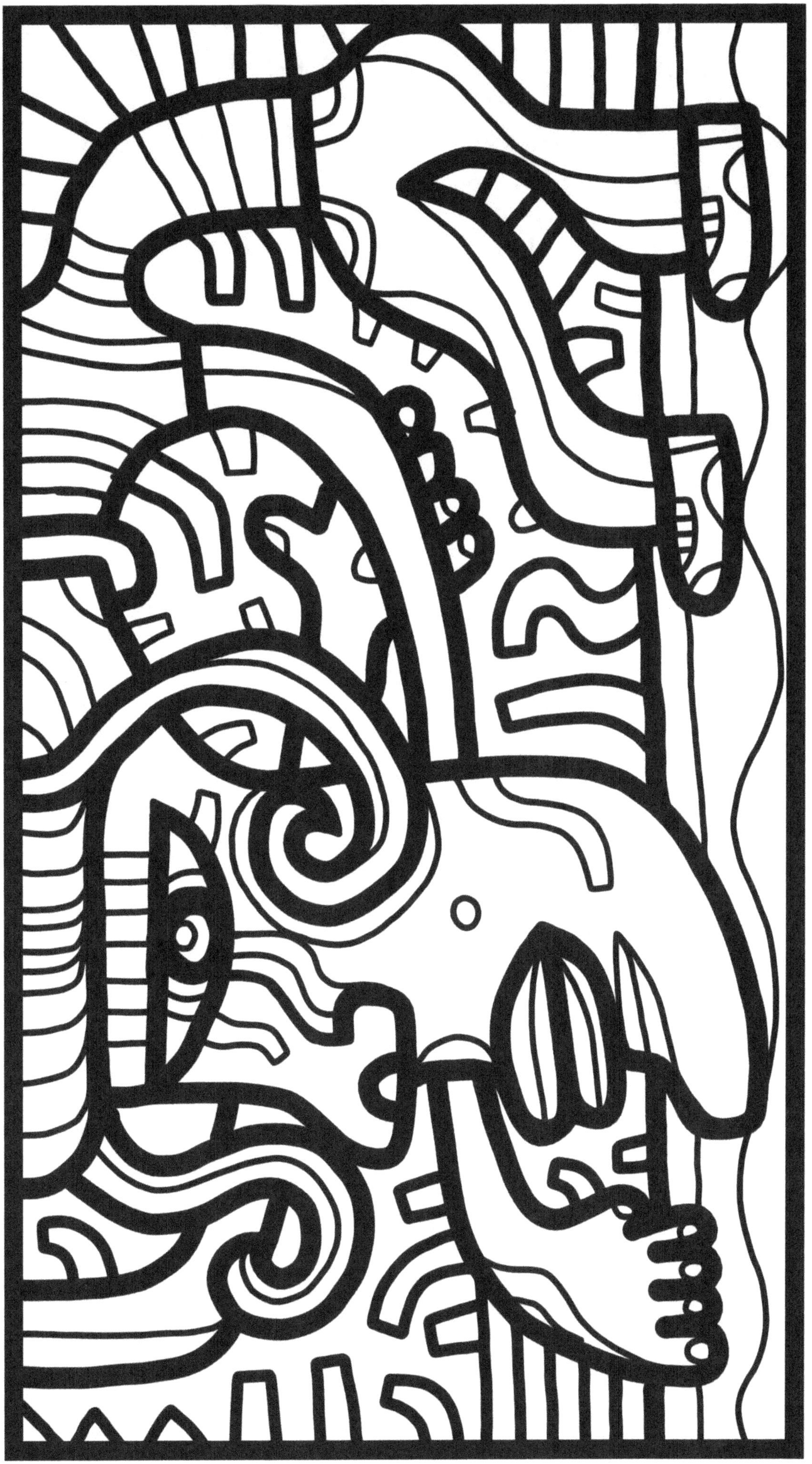

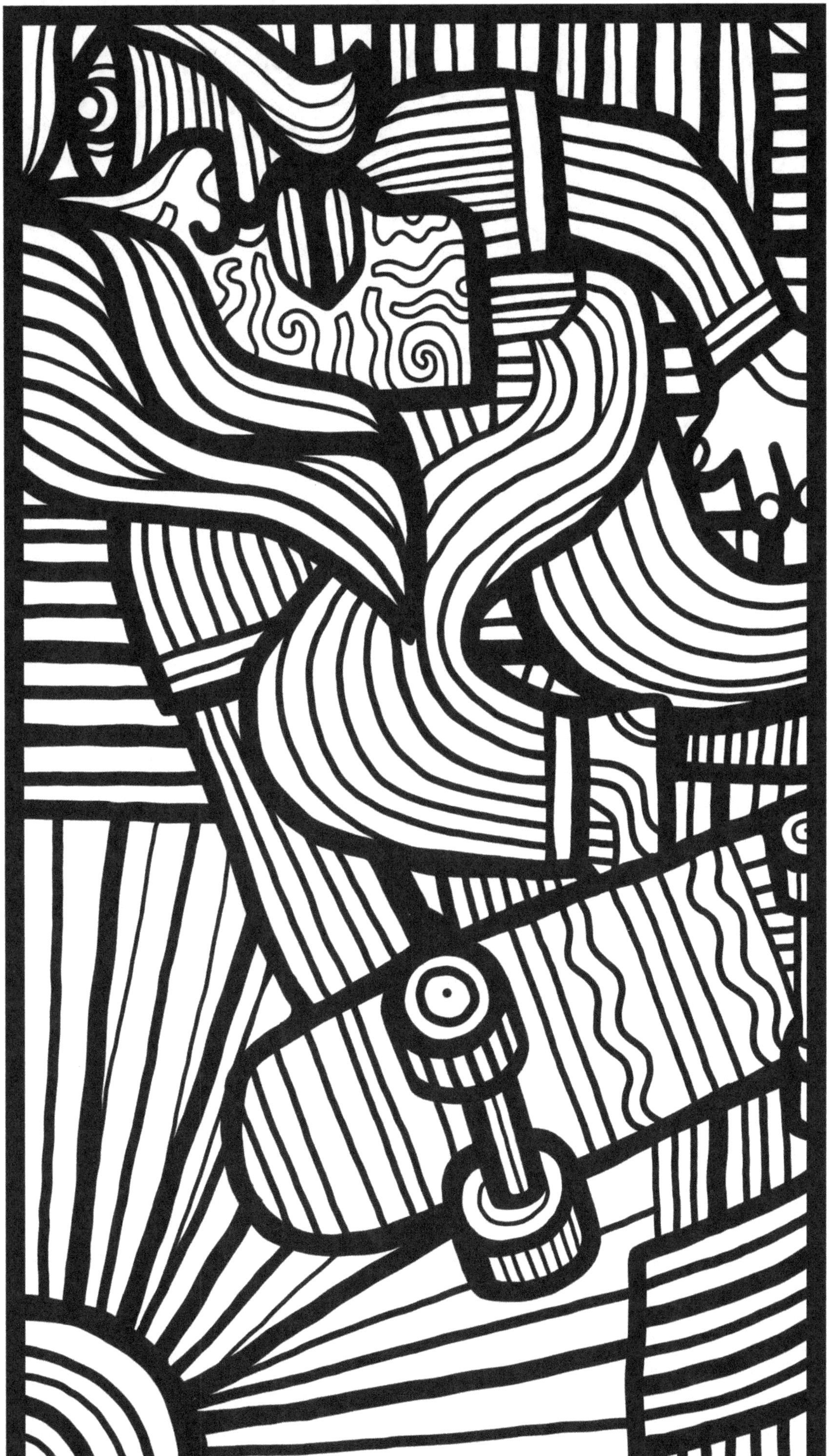

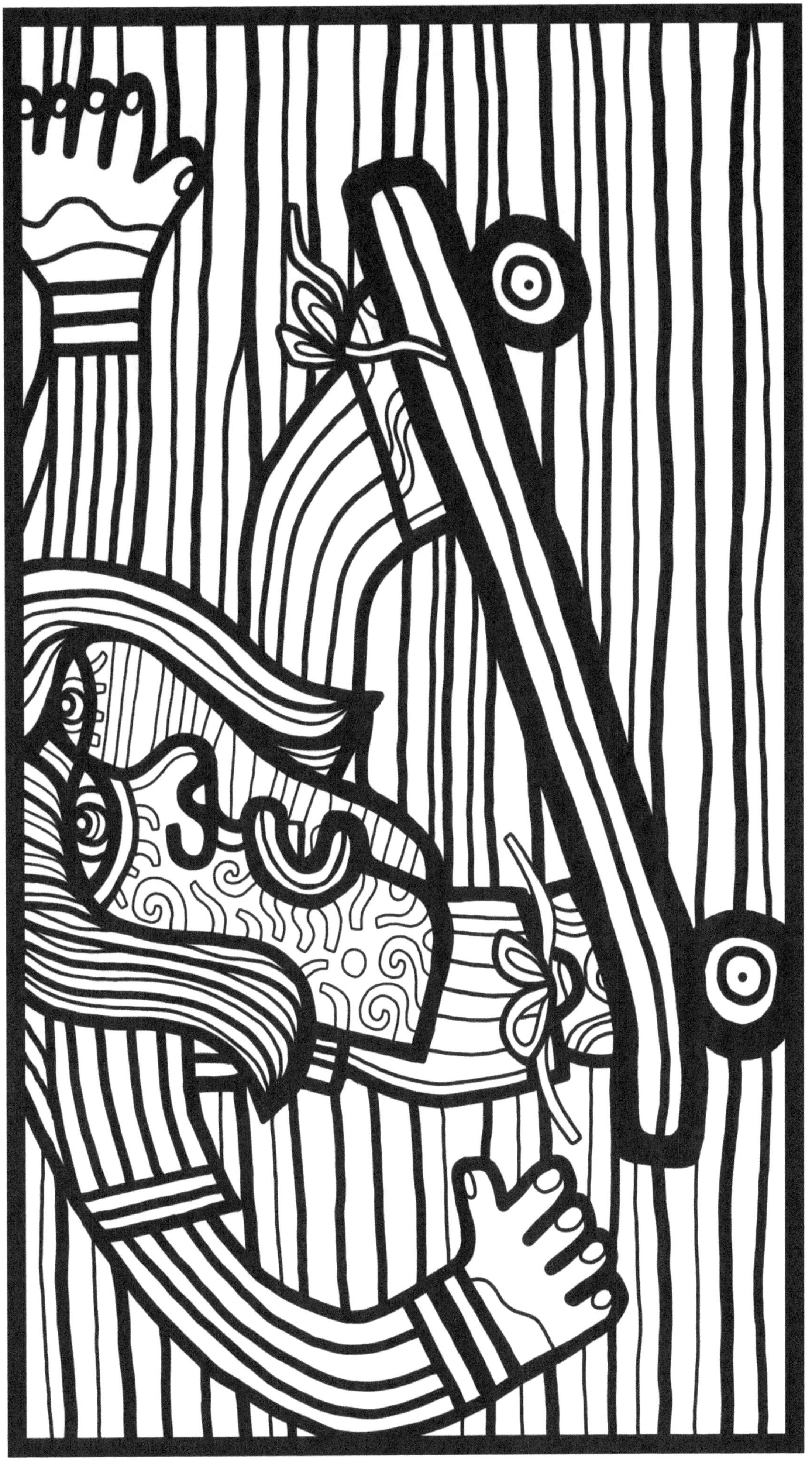

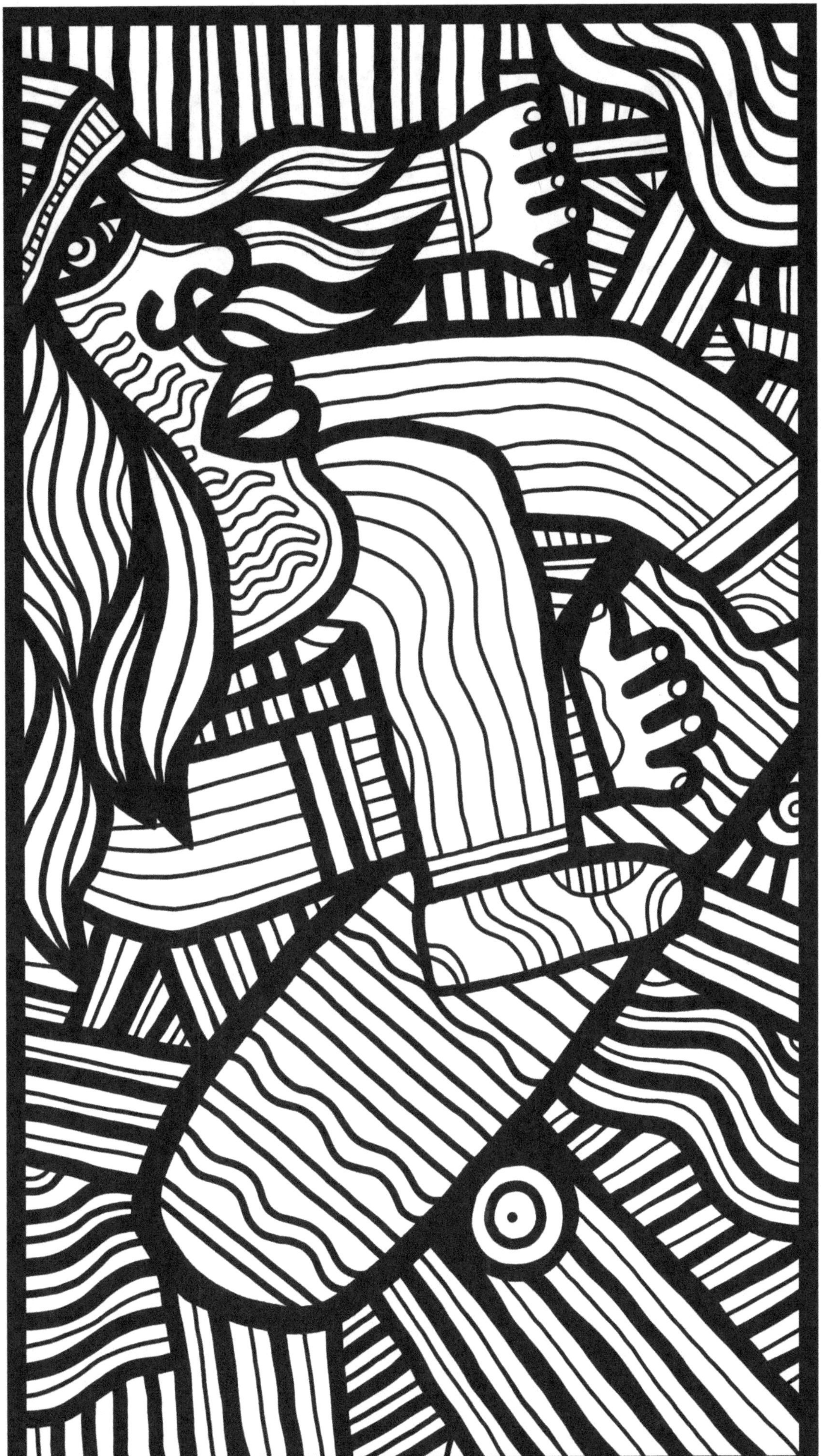

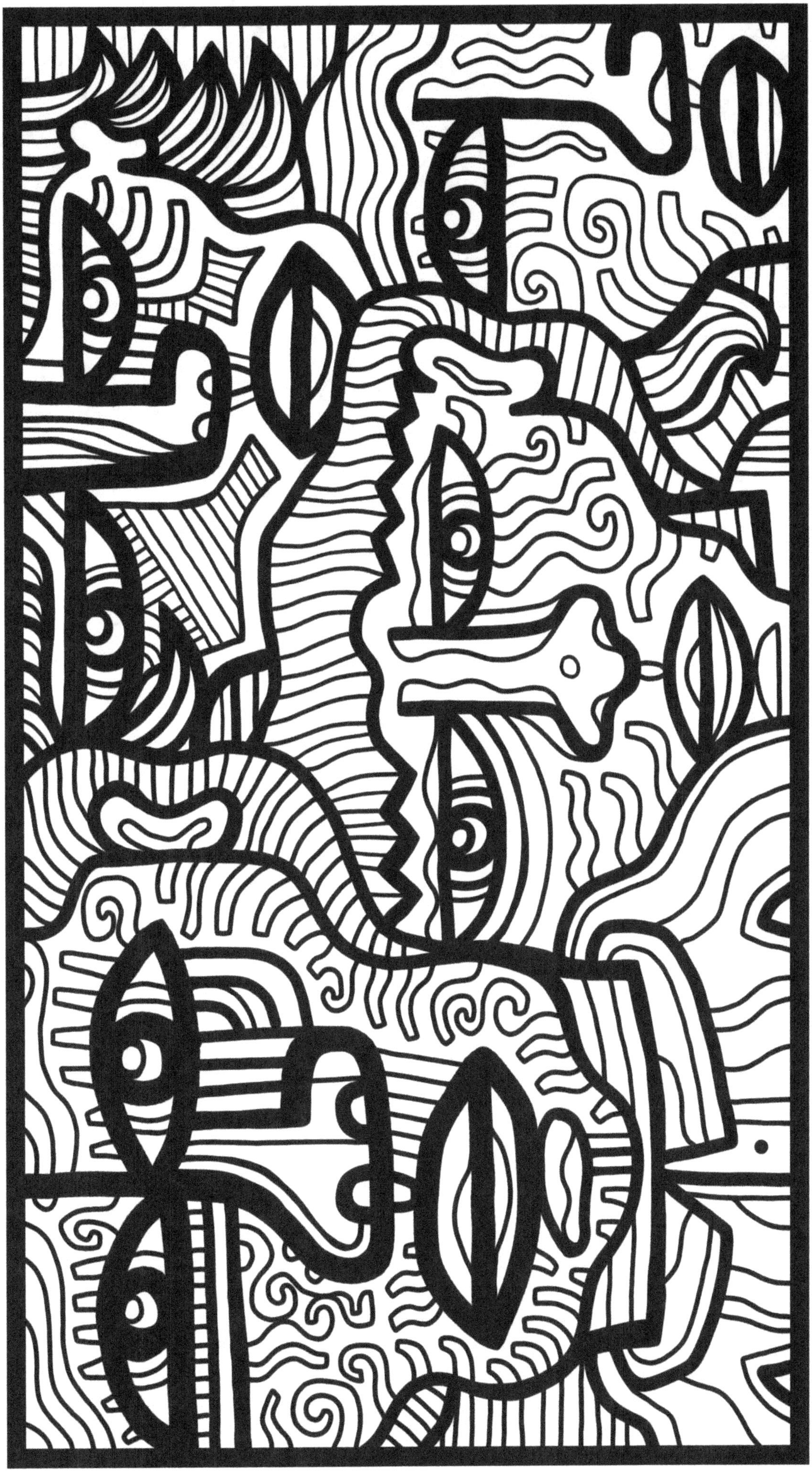

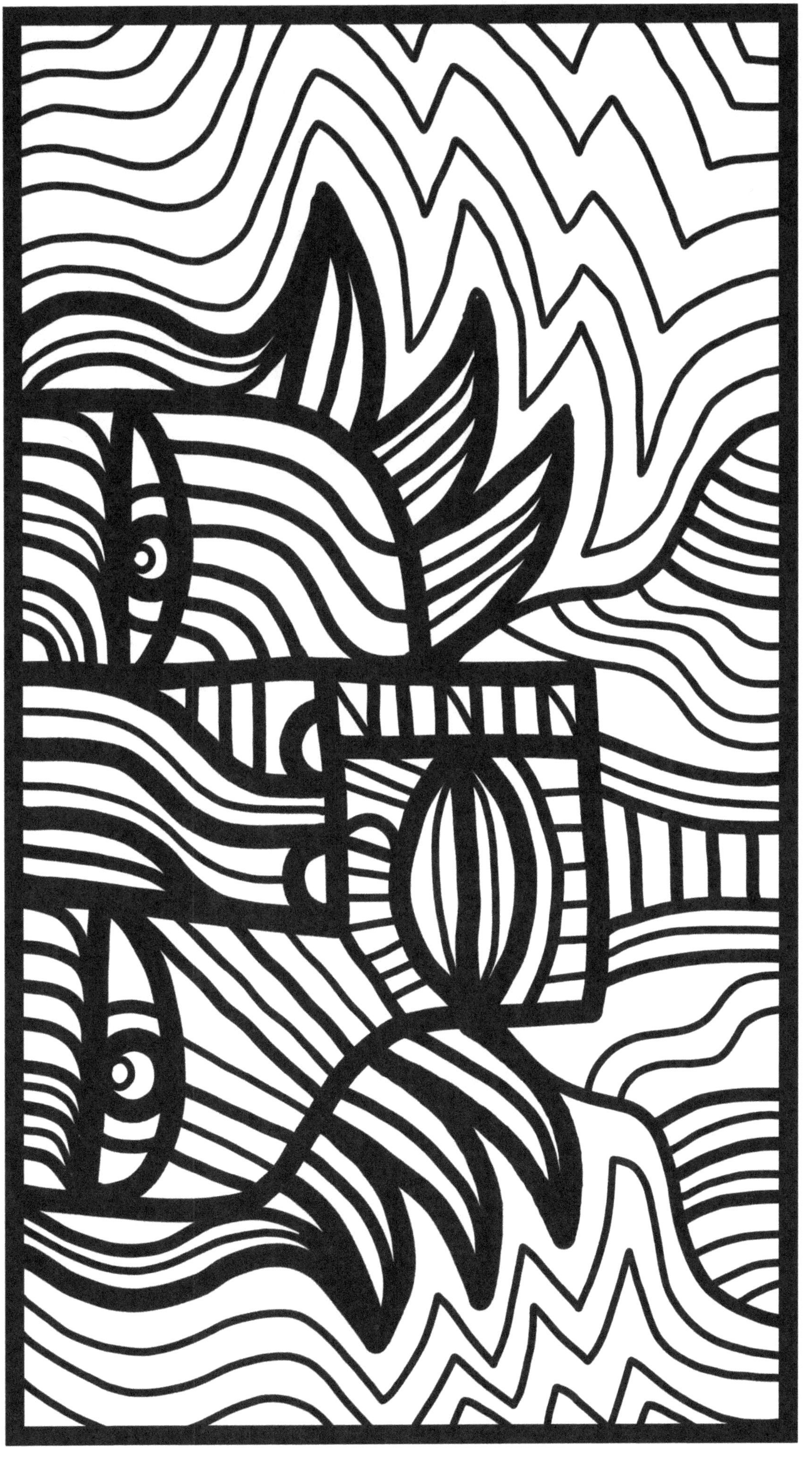

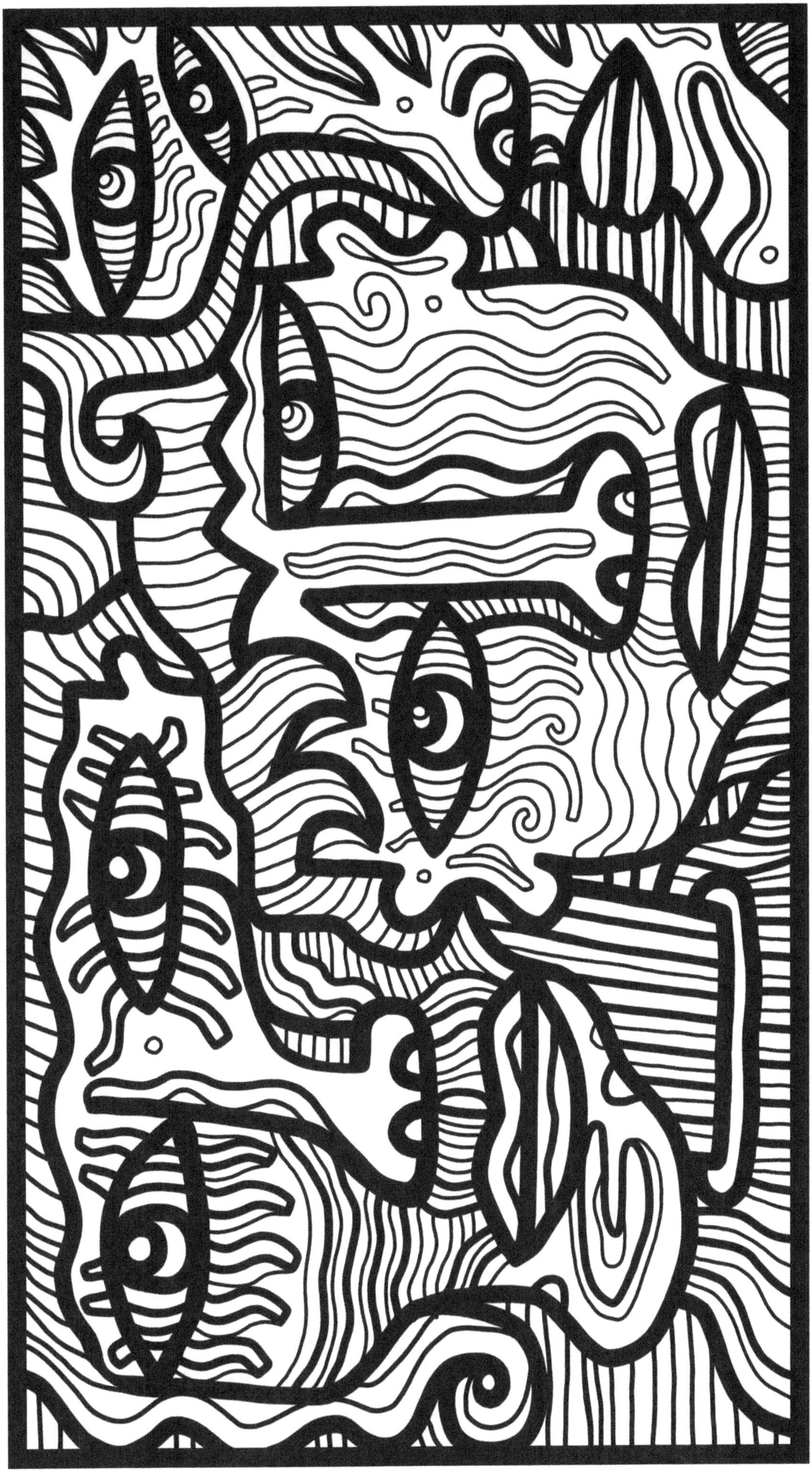

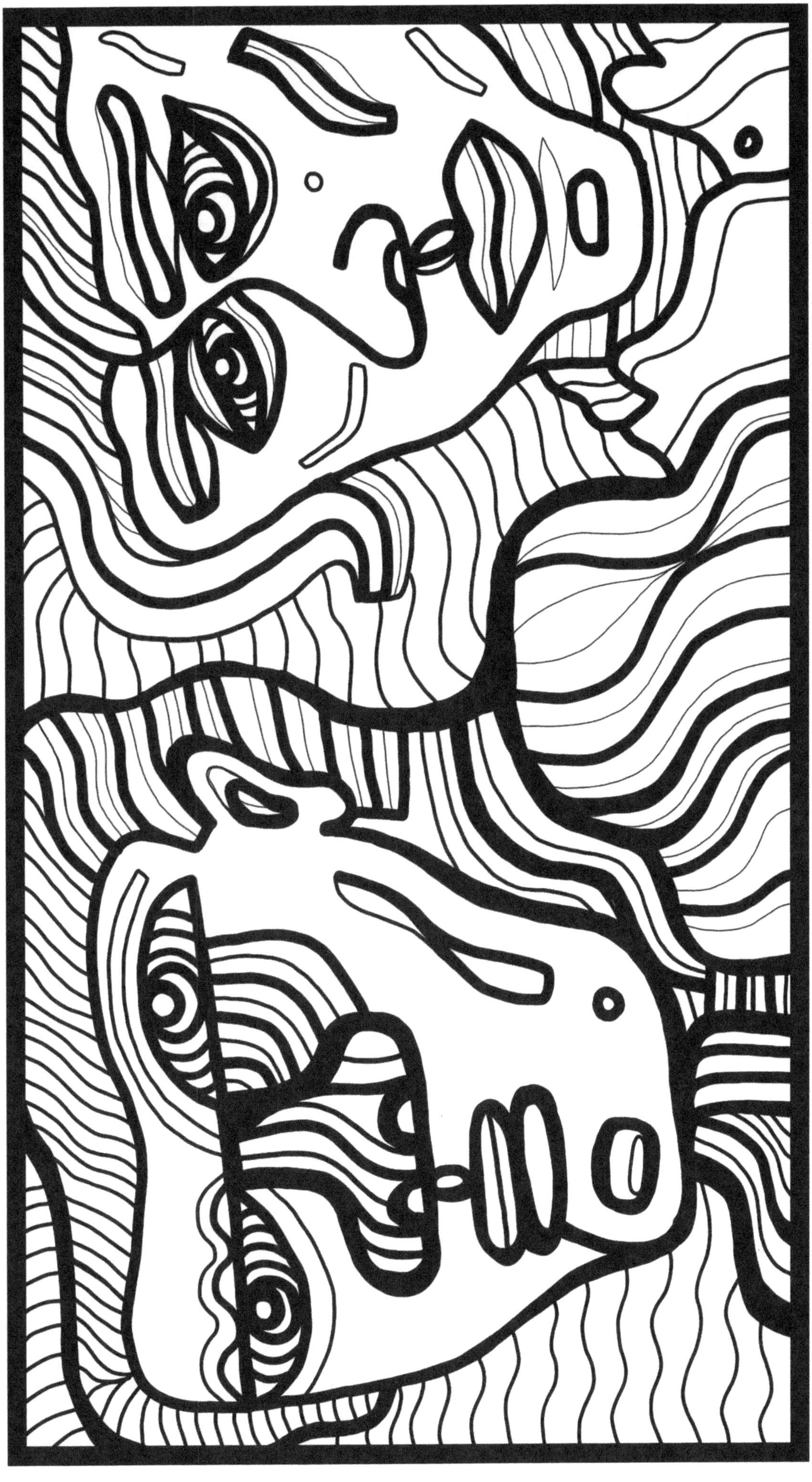

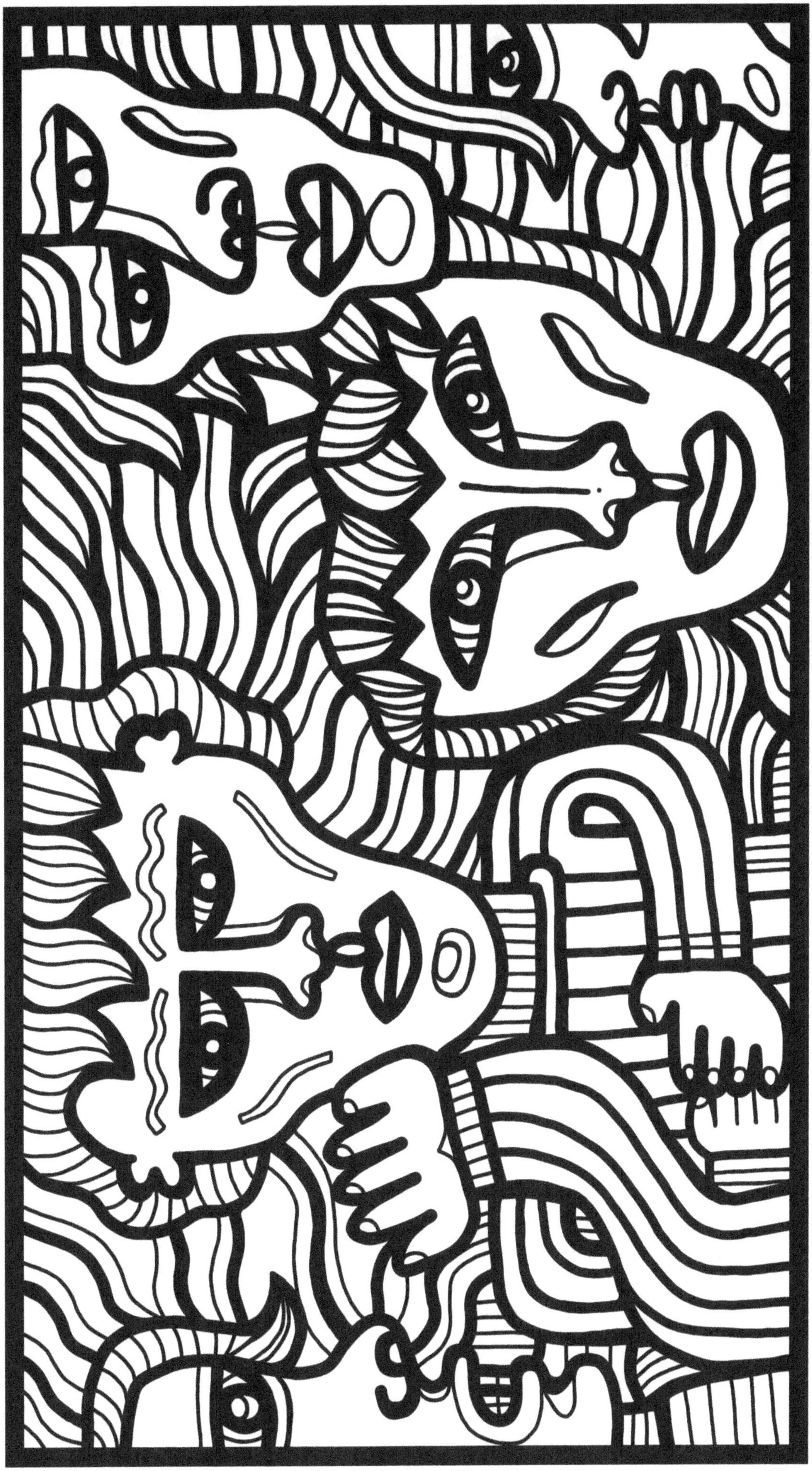

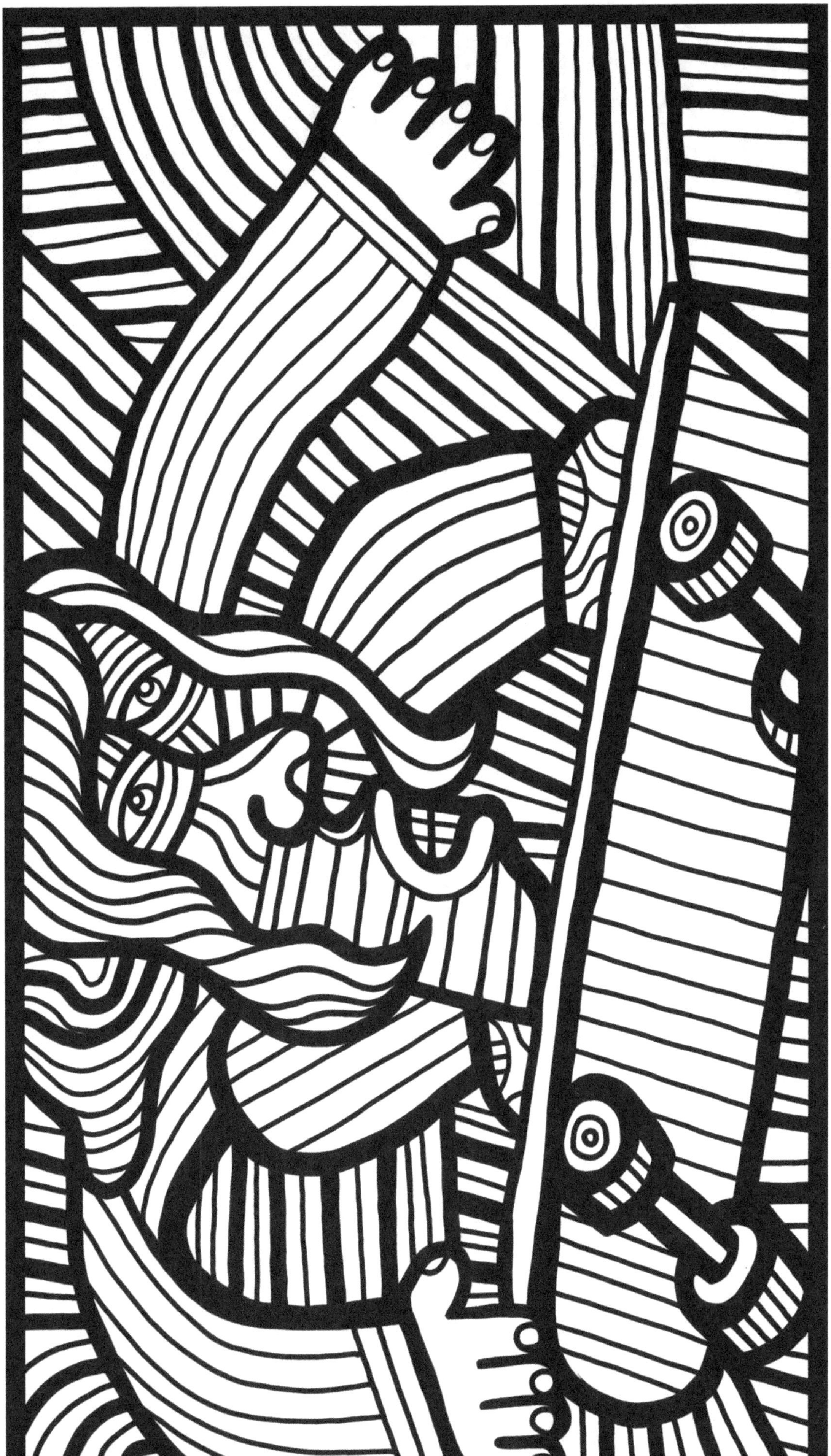

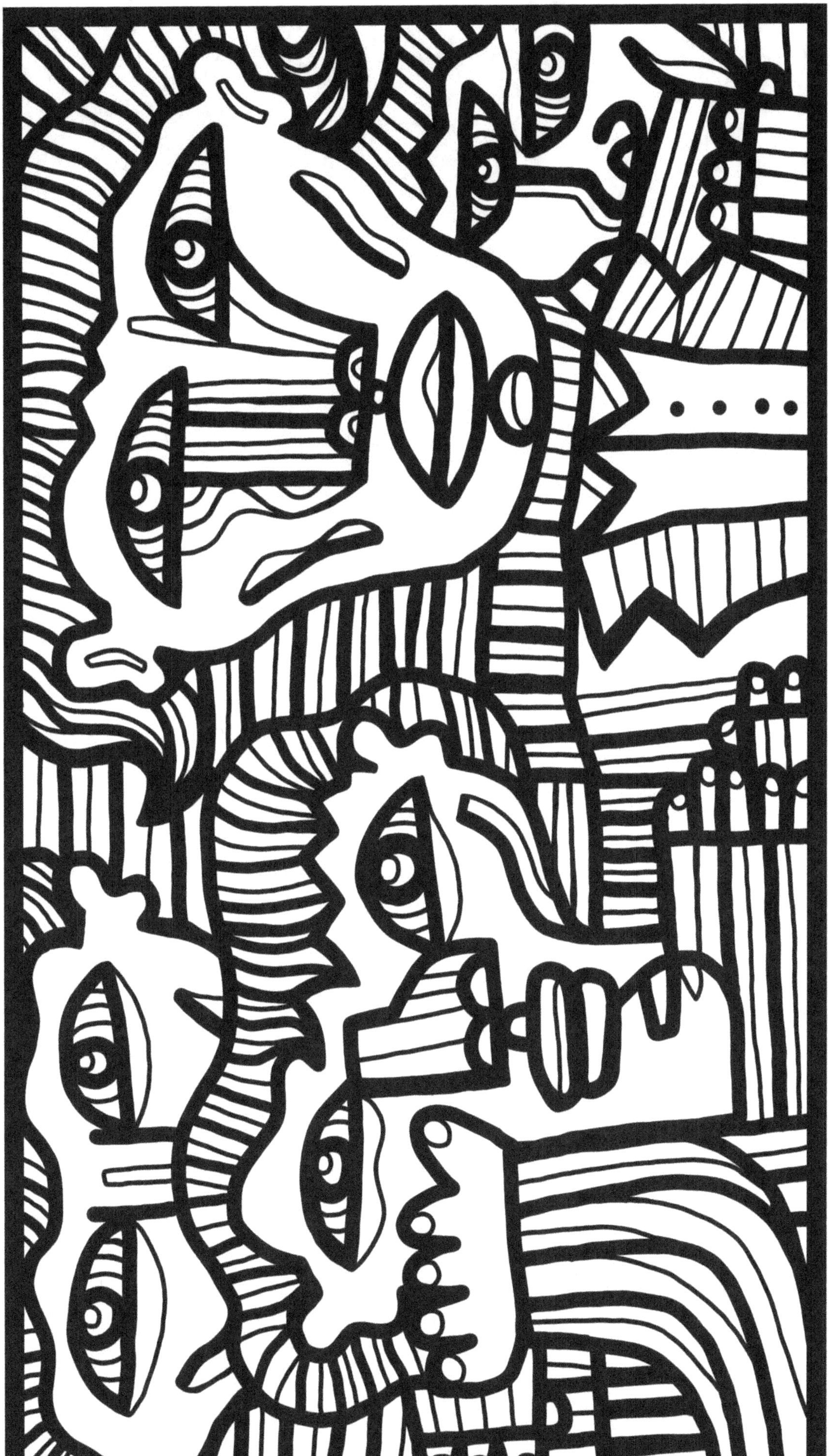

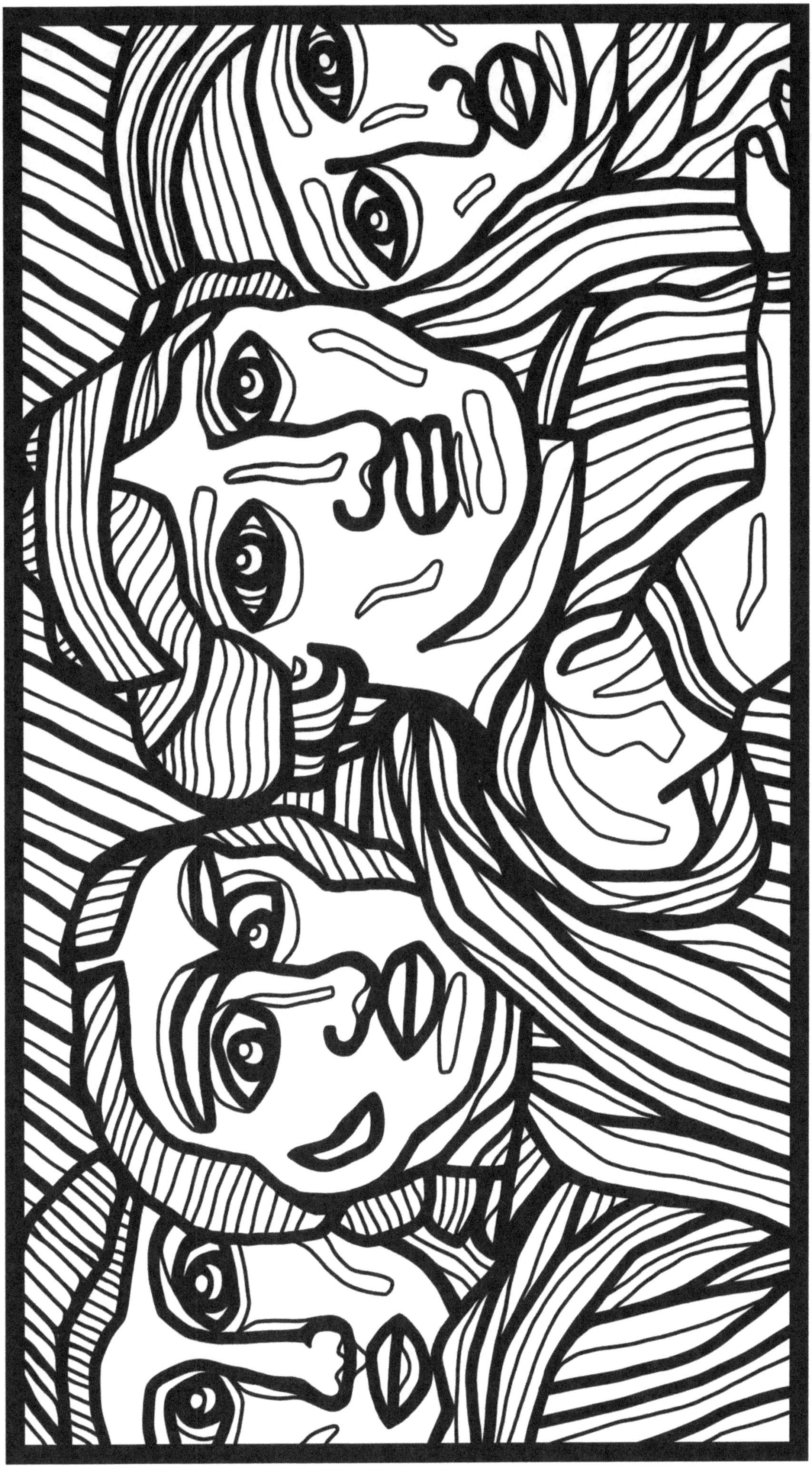

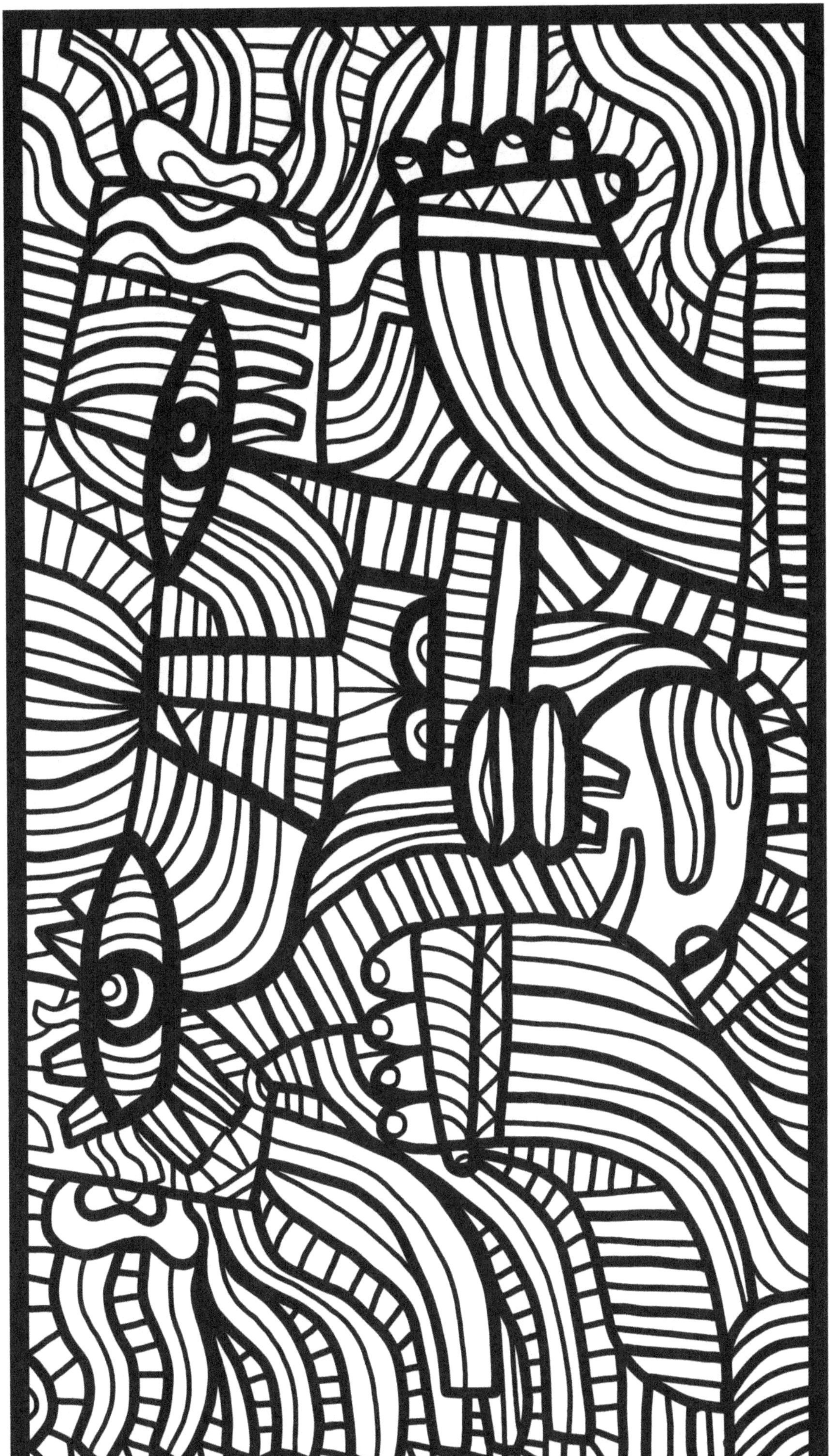

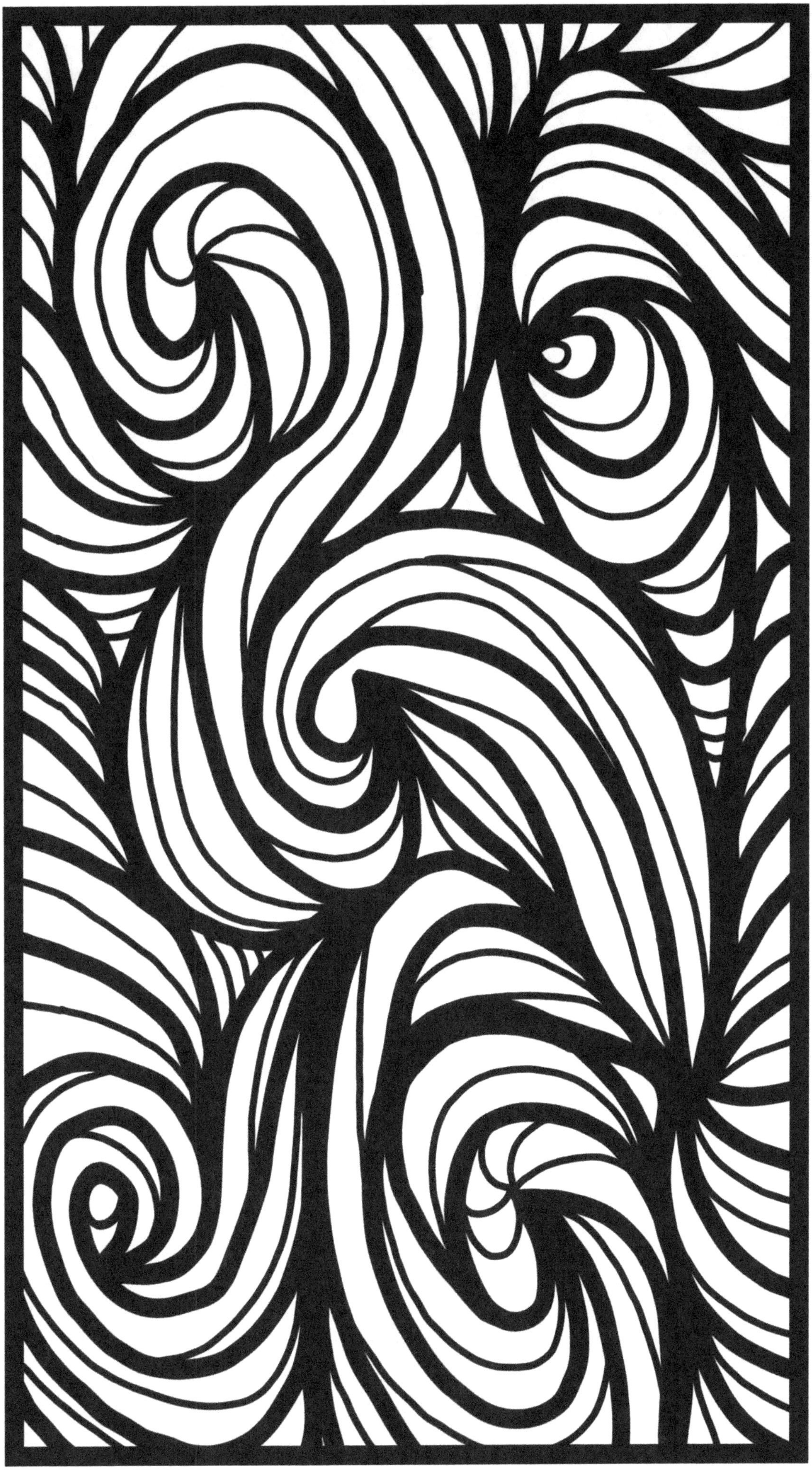

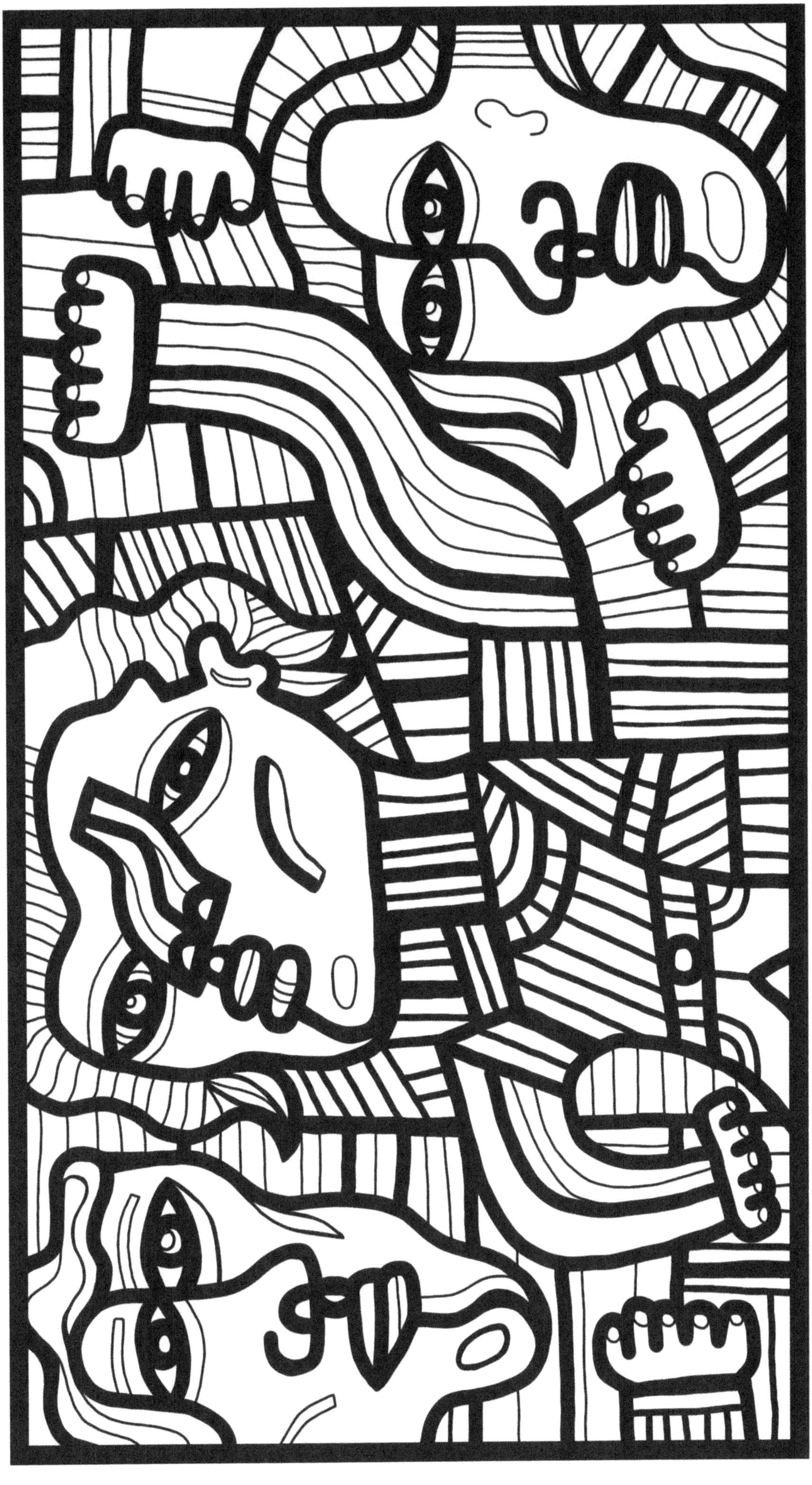

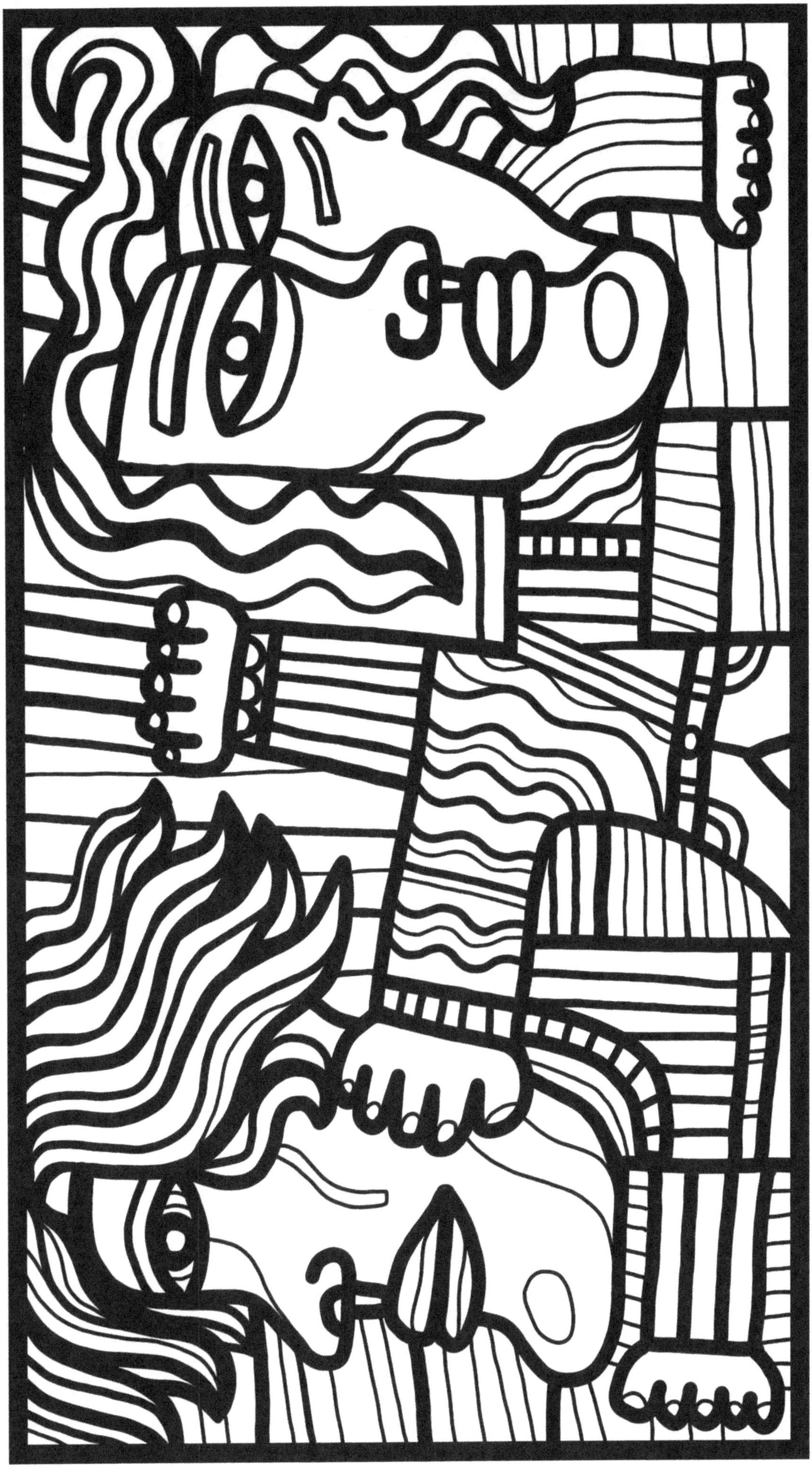

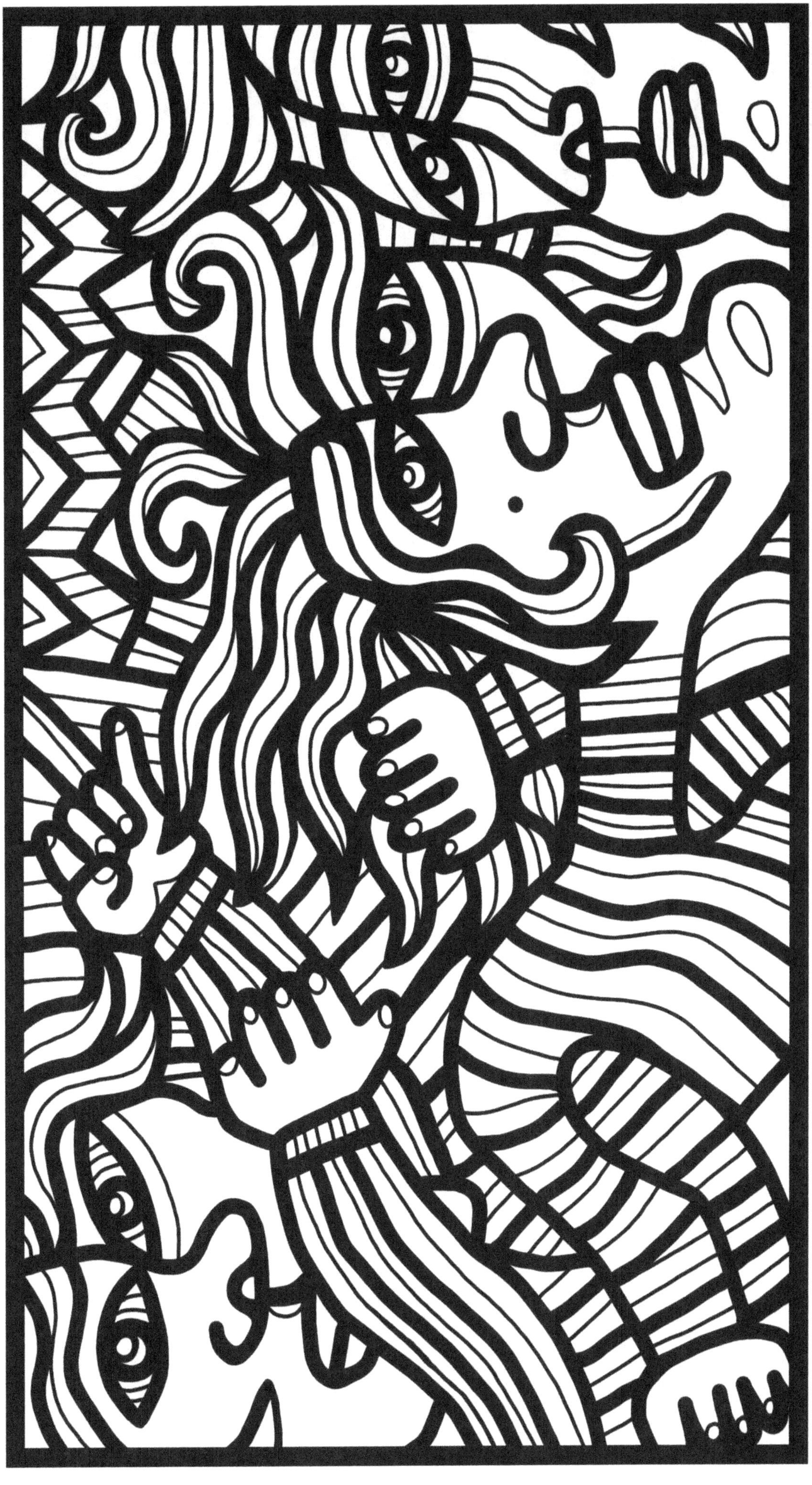

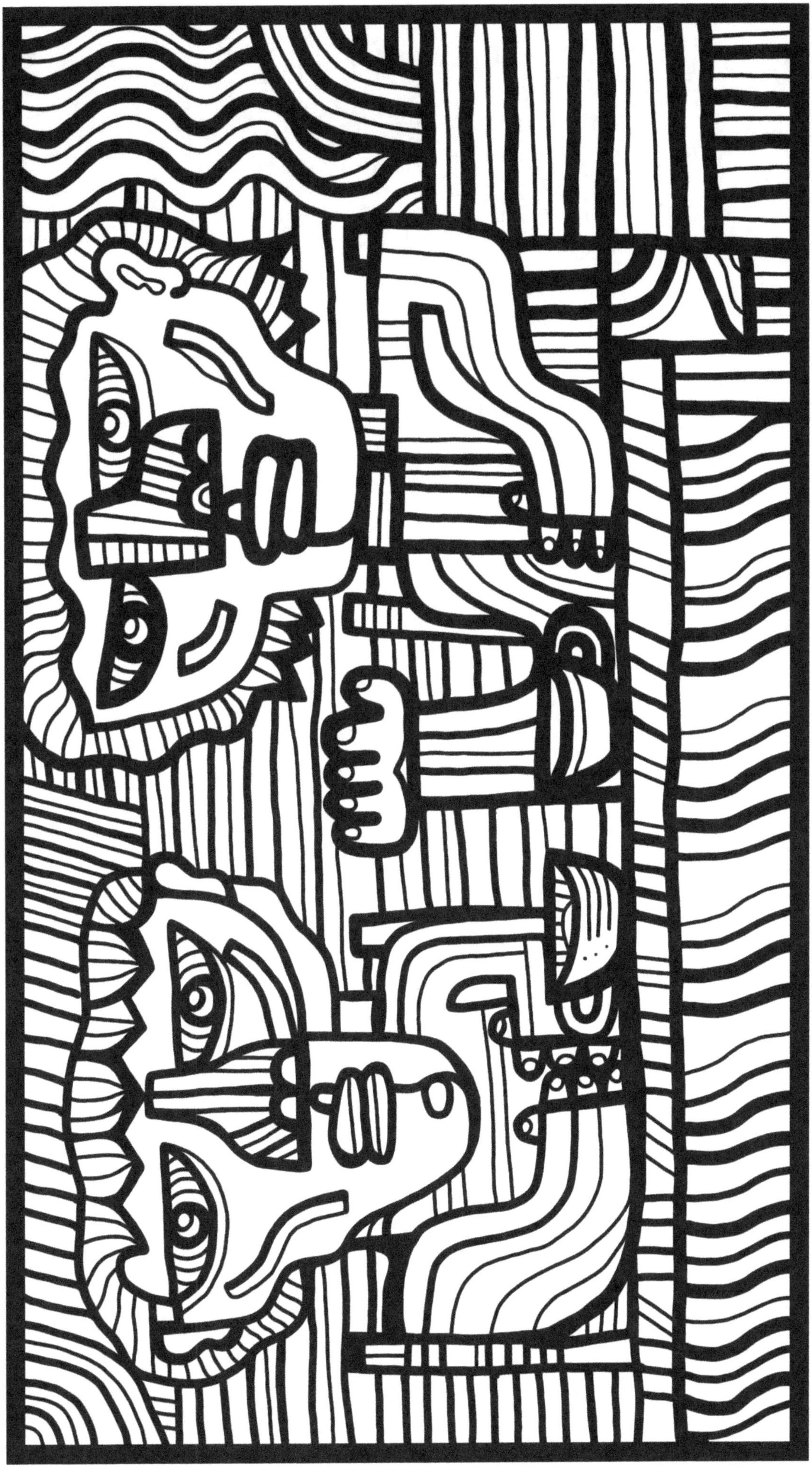

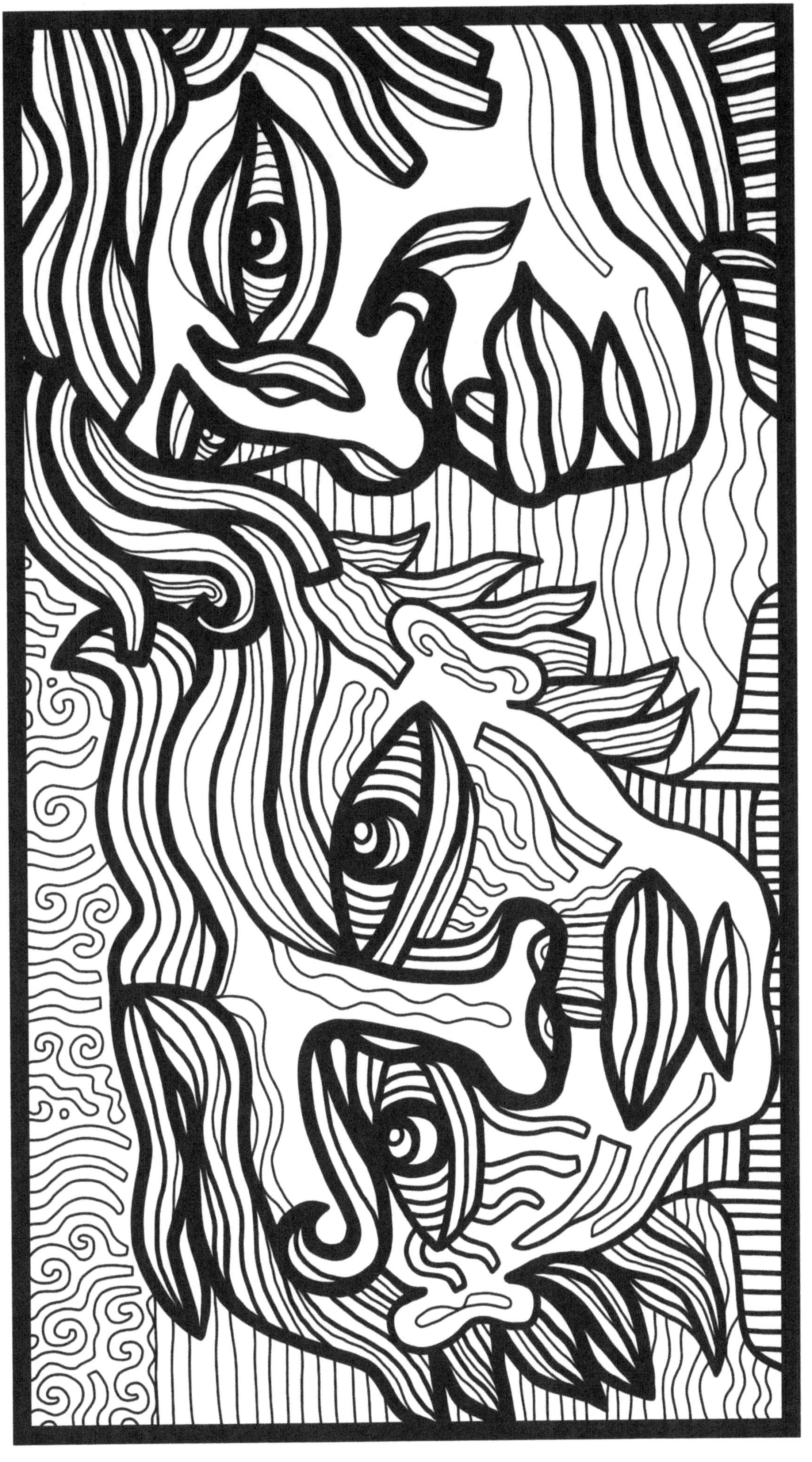

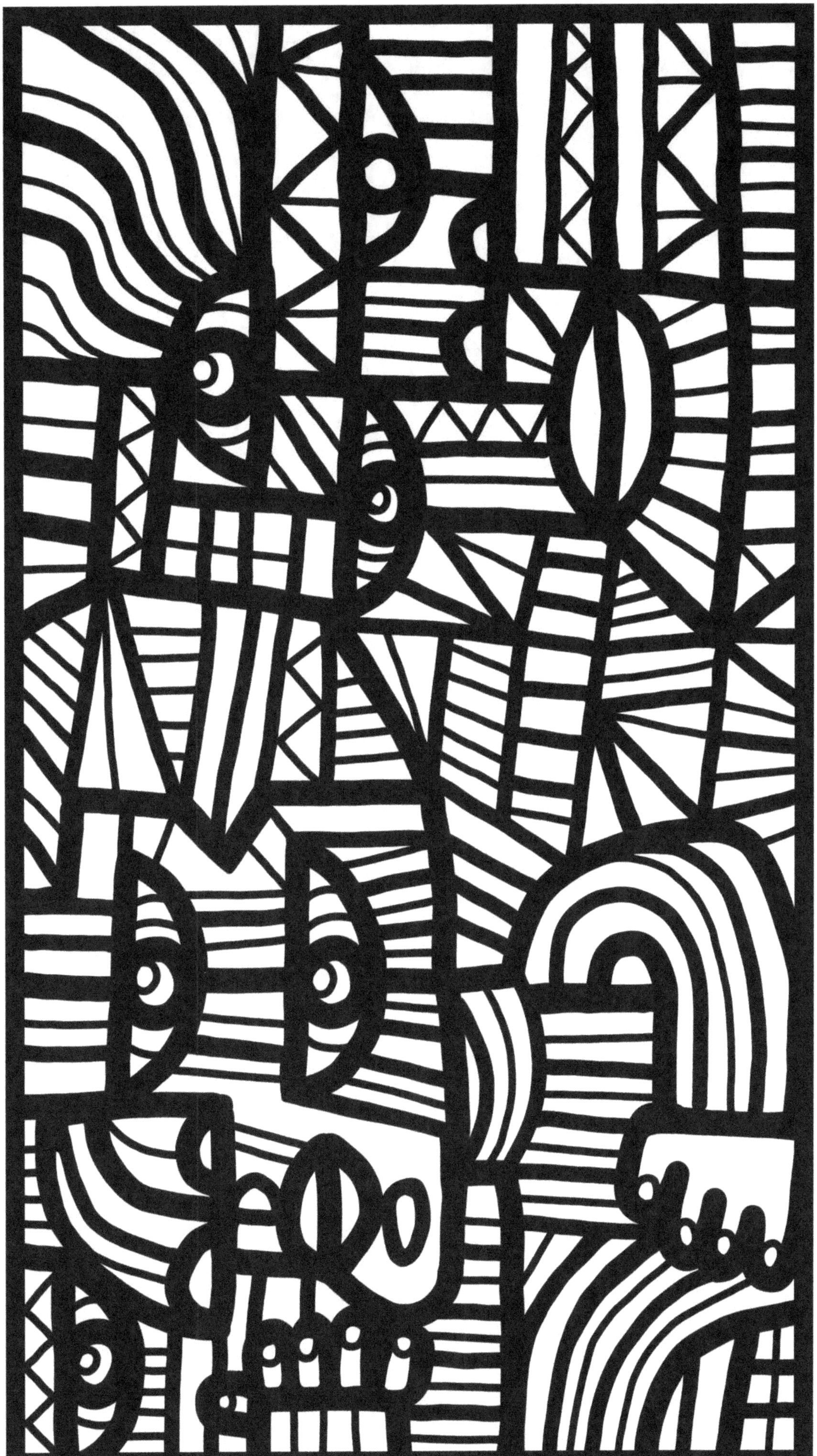

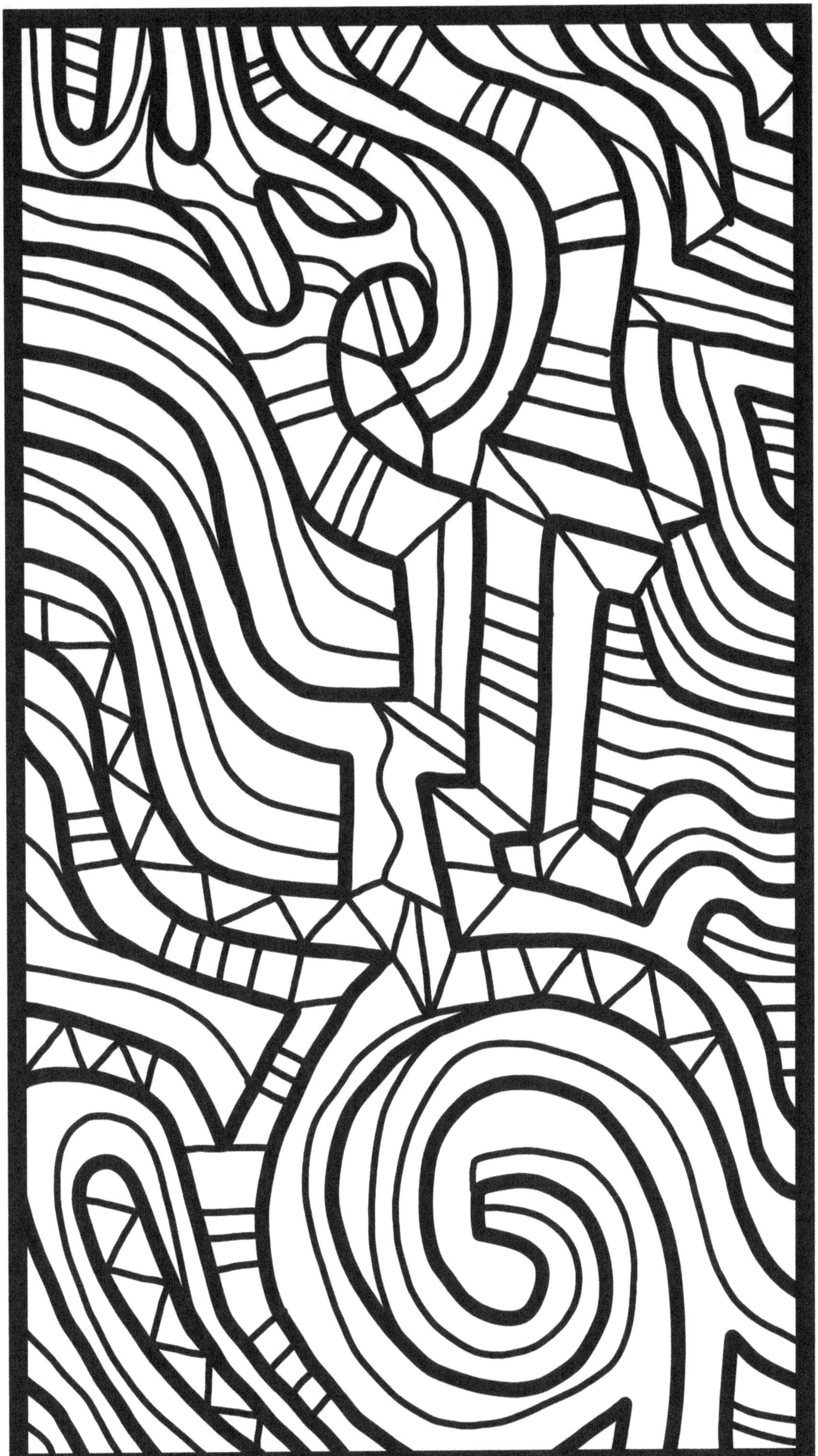

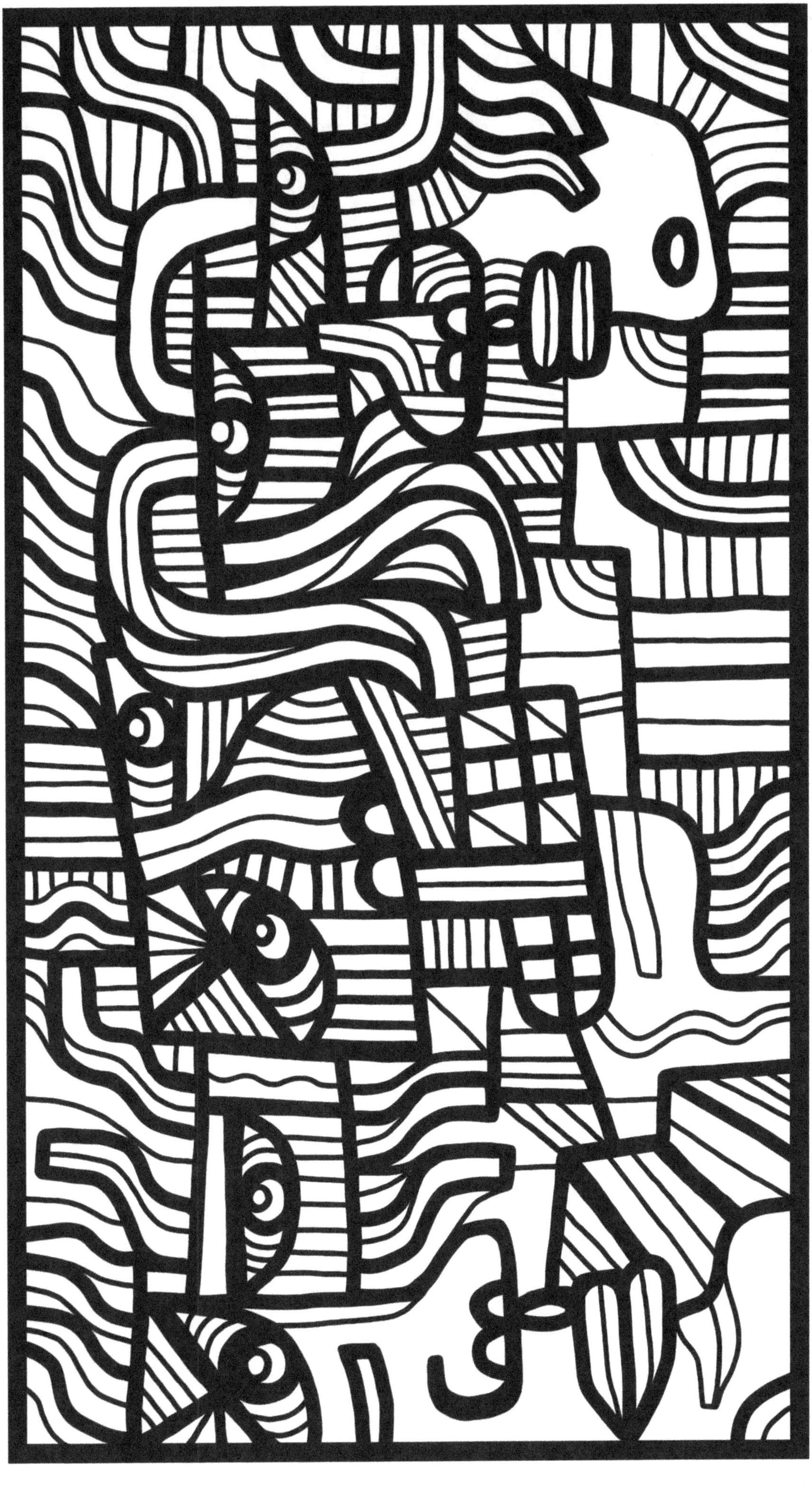

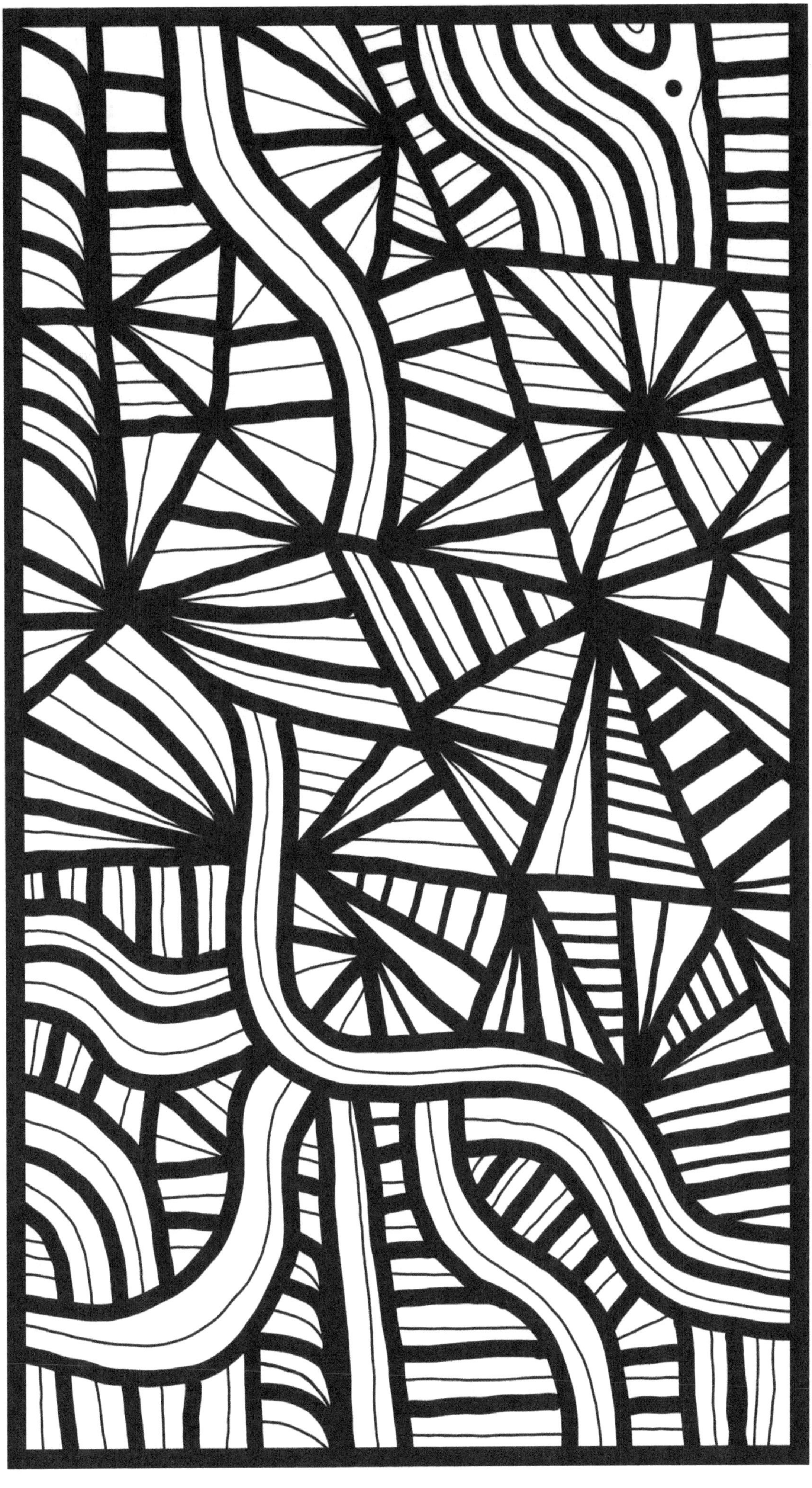

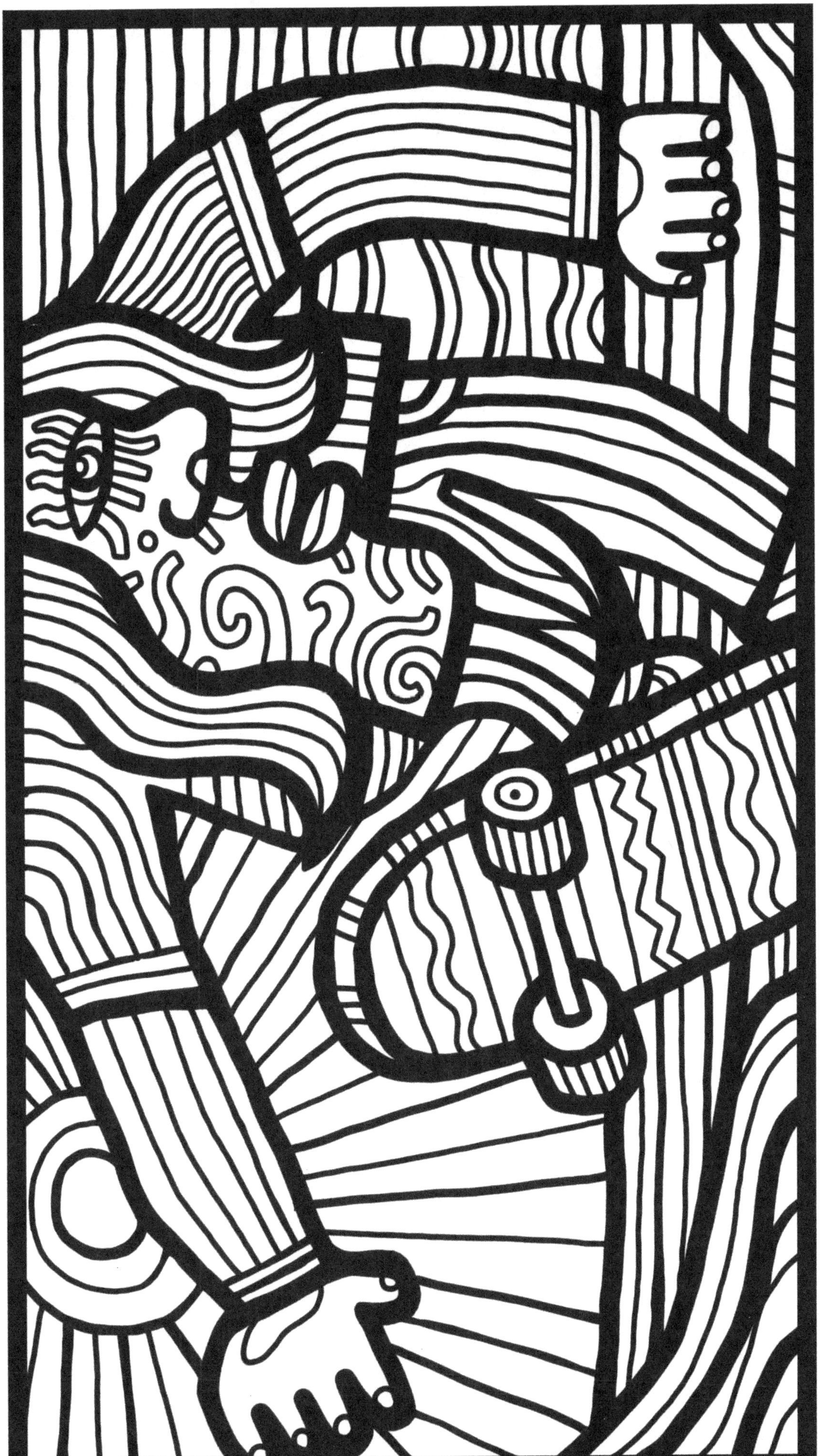

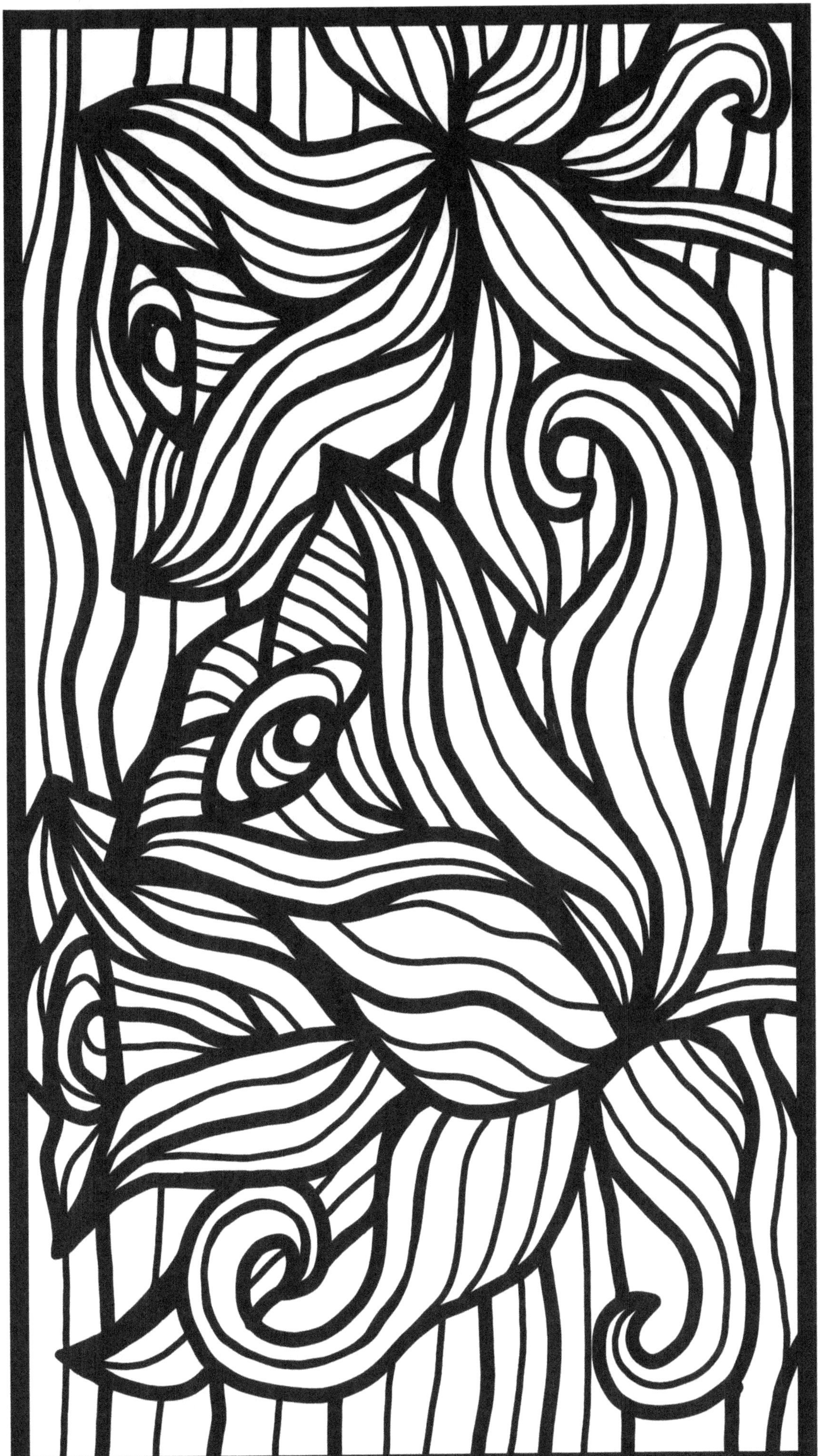

THE END, THANK YOU.

MORE BOOKS:
631ART.COM

www.ingramcontent.com/pod-product-compliance
Lightning Source LLC
Chambersburg PA
CBHW080134240526
45468CB00009BA/2426
* 9 7 8 1 7 9 5 6 0 9 7 5 3 *